REENTRY
AND
RESILIENCE

Supporting Formerly Incarcerated
Youth in Urban High Schools

DR. ROBERT E. GAINES

Reentry and Resilience: Supporting Formerly Incarcerated Youth in Urban High Schools

Copyright © 2025 by Dr. Robert E. Gaines

For more information, contact Dr. Robert E. Gaines at rgaines@wmsd.net.

Editing and Proofing Services: The Writing Doctor – thewritingdr.com

Book Publishing Consultant: Dr. Lorneka Joseph – drlorneka.co

Formatting: Ya Ya Ya Creative – yayayacreative@gmail.com

ISBN 979-8-9931890-0-0

PRINTED AND BOUND IN THE UNITED STATES OF AMERICA

Foreword

———————■———————

Dr. Robert Gaines, a seasoned educator and administrator with decades of experience in the Memphis Mid-South region, masterfully bridges traditional educational values with a modern, forward-thinking approach. In his insightful and instructional book, *Reentry and Resilience: Supporting Formerly Incarcerated Youth in Urban High Schools*, Dr. Gaines offers a transformative guide that speaks to students, parents, educators, and administrators across the nation.

Reading this book was a truly eye-opening experience. It issued a powerful call to action for all of us involved in the education and rehabilitation of youth who have experienced the juvenile justice system. These young people, ready to leave their past behind and forge new paths, often find themselves discouraged—not by a lack of will, but by the lack of systems and support necessary for their success. The puzzle pieces of opportunity are often missing, making it difficult for them to move forward in their educational journey.

Dr. Gaines draws from years of research and firsthand experience with issues like truancy and student behavioral challenges—two of the leading factors contributing to high school dropouts and juvenile incarceration. His work shines a light on the structural and systemic barriers that too often push students out, rather than help them stay in.

I firmly believe that all students—directly or indirectly—want to succeed. Our problem isn't a dropout crisis; it's a push-out crisis. *Reentry and Resilience* is the blueprint we need to help formerly incarcerated students reintegrate into our schools and communities, giving them the real chance they deserve to build better futures.

This book is more than just a guide—it is a bridge. A bridge from failure to success, from isolation to inclusion, and from lost potential to realized dreams.

–*Mr. Maurice Blair*

Table of Contents

—————————————◼—————————————

CHAPTER 1

Behind the Walls
Education in the
Shadow of Incarceration

JAMAL'S CLASSROOM

In the summer of 2012, Jamal sat in a windowless classroom inside the Westside Juvenile Detention Center. The room, painted in a sterile pale blue, smelled faintly of bleach and cafeteria food. A corrections officer stood near the door, arms folded, glancing at his watch more than the students. Jamal stared blankly at a worksheet labeled, "Algebra I—Week 3." At sixteen, he had already failed Algebra I twice before being arrested for fighting in school.

"This looks like something from middle school," he muttered.

The teacher, who was young, new and uncertified, gave no explanation for the assignment. Offering only a clipped response, he said, "just finish it by the end of the hour." Jamal picked up his pencil, not because he understood the work or felt motivated to try, but because it was easier than confrontation.

For students like Jamal, education in confinement was not a path forward, it was a holding pattern. The school inside the detention center, like many across the country, was under-resourced, disconnected from his home district, and poorly aligned with any meaningful graduation plan. No Individualized Education Plan (IEP) followed him here. There was no explanation of the credit recovery system while incarcerated. Jamal wasn't even sure if what he was doing counted toward his diploma.

THE SCHOOL-TO-PRISON PIPELINE

Over the past three decades, public schools, especially those in urban districts, have become tightly woven into the fabric of the juvenile justice system. The rise of zero-tolerance policies in the 1990s, fueled by fear of school violence, led to mandatory suspensions, expulsions, and arrests for behaviors once handled by counselors or principals.

National data show that Black students are more than three times more likely to be suspended or expelled as opposed to their white peers (U.S. Department of Education, 2018). Students with disabilities, those in foster care, and those experiencing homelessness are similarly overrepresented in exclusionary discipline actions.

The result? Thousands of students are pushed out of classrooms and into detention centers—many of which are ill-equipped to provide consistent, rigorous education. A growing body of research calls this phenomenon the *school-to-prison pipeline*.

WHAT HAPPENS INSIDE

When Jamal first arrived at Westside, he was told he'd attend school daily. What he found was something else entirely! Jamal received limited instructional time, a revolving door of teachers, and classroom materials that were years out of date.

Jamal was placed in a "combined" classroom with youth ages 14–18. All the students were different grade levels with different educational needs. Lessons were worksheet-based, focused more on control than instruction. Students who acted out were removed from class. Students like Jamal, who were quiet and compliant, were passed through the system with little academic progress.

Jamal later described his experience in an interview. See below:

"It was like they just wanted us to be quiet. They didn't care if we learned anything. They didn't even tell me if my credits counted. I felt like I was just doing time."

THE DISCONNECT UPON REENTRY

Six months later, Jamal returned to Yellowtail High School. The return was unceremonious. He re-enrolled with the help of his grandmother, who had raised him since he was ten.

Upon arrival back to his former high school, no meeting was held and no counselor greeted him. No one seemed to know where Jamal had been or what to do next. Jamal was handed a schedule with classes he had already failed and told to "just do better this time."

The academic counselor, overwhelmed with a caseload of 300 students, later admitted, "We don't get any information from the juvenile centers, if a kid comes back, it's like starting from scratch."

Within two months, Jamal was failing three classes. He skipped more and more days and by the end of the semester, he dropped out completely.

A BROKEN SYSTEM OF SUPPORT

Jamal's story is not unique. It is emblematic of a deeply fractured system. Youth who return from incarceration face the following significant obstacles:

- Gaps in academic credit

- Lack of mental health services

- Stigma from peers and staff

- Pressure to support family financially

- Disengagement due to repeated school failure

The system is meant to support reentry. Education, juvenile justice and mental health often work in silos. While federal law requires some educational continuity, enforcement is inconsistent, especially in underfunded urban school districts.

SETTING THE STAGE

This book is about those young people, like Jamal, and the educators, counselors, families, and administrators trying to help them navigate hostile terrain. It is also about the policies and structures that make their success unnecessarily harder.

We begin here, behind the walls, because that is where the educational journey of many of these students breaks down. What happens inside detention centers and how schools respond when students return, sets the trajectory for everything that follows.

The chapters ahead explore the experiences of stakeholders who have lived and worked through the reentry process. Their voices are clear: we can do better. Through narratives, research, and the development of the **FIRST Plan**, this book proposes a roadmap for making our schools more ready and more just for every student who deserves a second chance.

STUDENT REFLECTIONS FROM INSIDE

Though Jamal's story is central to this chapter, other students shared similar experiences of isolation and frustration with education behind bars.

"We didn't have real classes," said Dante (17). Dante spent four months in a county juvenile facility. "It was all packets. Same ones every week. Nobody explained anything."

Amira, 16, who had been incarcerated for a probation violation, recalled feeling invisible in her classroom. Amira said, "The teacher never said my name once, just dropped a worksheet and walked away. I wasn't a student, I was an inmate doing time."

Tyrell, who returned to Yellowtail High after serving eight months, described the contrast between the facility's classroom and the public school system:

"In there, the rules were simple—be quiet, stay in line, do your work. Out here, it's chaos. Nobody tells you what's expected, but they still expect you to keep up."

These voices reveal how education in confinement is often transactional and punitive, rather than supportive or transformative. Many students described the classroom in detention centers not as a place of growth, but as another tool of control.

"They'd say school was a privilege, but it felt more like punishment," said Lashawn.

A BROKEN PROMISE OF EDUCATION

Public education is often described as the "great equalizer," a pathway to opportunity regardless of background. However, for youth inside the juvenile justice system, education often functions as a locked door instead of a ladder. Instead of an opportunity, they receive worksheets, temporary staffing, and environments focused more on compliance than learning.

In many juvenile detention centers, instruction is minimal. Students are assigned packets of basic material, often below grade level, and left to work independently.

"We got the same packet three times, they changed the date on the front," said Lamar (15).

These students are not treated as learners, they're treated as liabilities.

EDUCATORS ON THE INSIDE

Facility-based educators often lack the training or resources to teach students with trauma, special needs, or disrupted learning histories.

"I had no curriculum," said one teacher from a county youth center. "I bought materials out of pocket. We couldn't use internet, so I was teaching GED prep with a chalkboard."

Staff turnover is high. Many classrooms go without certified teachers for weeks. Students with IEPs are rarely served according to their plans. The legal requirement to provide education becomes, in practice, a paper exercise.

A SYSTEM WITHIN A SYSTEM

Juvenile education is governed by a patchwork of state and local policies, with no national standard for quality or access. Some youth are detained in centers run by their school district. Others are placed in facilities administered by corrections departments or private vendors. The result is a vast inconsistency to what "education" looks like from one facility to another.

This inconsistency affects minorities the most, specifically Black, Latino, and low-income youth, who are disproportionately incarcerated. According to federal data, Black youth make up 15% of the U.S. adolescent population but over 35% of youth in juvenile detention. These racialized patterns mirror those seen in school suspensions and expulsions, suggesting not random contact with the justice system, but systemic design.

THE MISSED OPPORTUNITY

Ironically, for some students, incarceration is the first time they attend school regularly. Instead of building on that moment, many facilities offer only remediation, compliance, and survival.

One mother said, "He was finally going to class, but he wasn't learning anything. He was just filling in blanks."

THE HANDOFF THAT DOESN'T HAPPEN

When students are released, there is rarely a coordinated plan between the facility and the receiving school. Transcripts are delayed or incomplete. Academic records are unclear. Mental health needs are undocumented. The student, once again, must navigate the system alone.

One school counselor said, "I asked what he did in there?" She was told, "We don't know, he'll figure it out when he gets here."

FROM THE SHADOWS TO THE HALLWAYS

This chapter lifts the curtain on how education operates behind the walls. This is not to vilify facility staff, but to expose a system built to contain, not uplift. Understanding this context is crucial, because it sets the stage for what happens next. Next, the student returns to a traditional classroom. The question that haunts every student and every parent is, "What are they returning to and who's waiting to receive them?"

CHAPTER 2

The Landscape of Disconnection
A Review of the Literature

"I JUST FELL OFF THE MAP"

After returning home from juvenile detention, Shania tried to enroll back into school. However, when she and her aunt went to the school office, the registrar handed them a thick packet and said, "We don't have your records, try the alternative school downtown." Shania never made it there.

"It felt like they didn't want me back, like I didn't exist in their system anymore," she later confessed in an interview.

Shania's experience reflects a broader truth; youth returning from incarceration often fall into a gap between institutions where no one is quite responsible for ensuring their education continues. This chapter reviews the research and policy literature that helps us understand how and why this disconnection happens, and what might be done to address it.

YOUTH INCARCERATION IN THE UNITED STATES

Each year, an estimated 48,000 youth are held in juvenile facilities across the country (OJJDP, 2023). The majority are Black, Latinx, or Indigenous. The average length of stay is between three to six months, but disruptions to schooling can last far longer. Some students are held pretrial for weeks or months without formal schooling. Others attend education programs in detention centers that don't offer credit transfers or meet state curriculum standards.

According to the National Juvenile Defender Center (2020), only 14 states require students in juvenile facilities to receive educational services equivalent to those in public schools. Even fewer ensure those students earn transferable credit toward high school graduation.

EDUCATIONAL DISRUPTION AND LEARNING LOSS

A consistent finding in the literature is the extent to which incarceration interrupts academic progress. Students often miss critical instruction, are placed in remedial or mixed-grade classrooms, and lose touch with educational goals. Even in facilities with education programs, instruction is often limited by staffing shortages, lack of certified teachers, inadequate materials, and/or security-driven interruptions.

One study by Houchins et al. (2017) found that students in juvenile facilities gained fewer than two months of reading growth during a full academic year in detention centers. In math, gains were even smaller. These disruptions compound when students return to schools that are unprepared to assess their current level and place them appropriately.

BARRIERS TO REENTRY IN SCHOOL SYSTEMS

The literature identifies multiple barriers to successful school reentry for formerly incarcerated youth:

- **Lack of coordination between agencies:** Juvenile justice, education, and social services often do not communicate. As a result, student records, IEPs, and academic transcripts are delayed or lost.

- **Stigma and labeling:** Students returning from detention centers are often viewed as troublemakers. Teachers may expect poor behavior and peer relationships can be strained.

- **Unclear enrollment procedures:** Many schools redirect returning students to alternative campuses or require extensive documentation that families may not be able to produce.

- **Mental health needs:** Youth often experience trauma during incarceration and return home without adequate psychological support.

These challenges are particularly acute in urban high schools, where staff are overburdened, resources limited, and school climates may already be strained by discipline issues and high dropout rates.

SCHOOL DISCIPLINE AND RACIAL DISPARITIES

Much of the literature on the school-to-prison pipeline emphasizes the role of school discipline practices in fueling disconnection. Zero-tolerance policies, in-school arrests, and out-of-school suspensions disproportionately affect students of color, particularly Black boys and students with disabilities.

Fabelo et al. (2011) demonstrated that a single suspension in middle or high school significantly increases the likelihood of contact with the juvenile justice system. Once in that system, the path to educational reengagement becomes steeper.

This is compounded by structural racism: schools in predominantly Black and Latinx communities tend to have fewer counselors, less experienced teachers, and more school police officers. When support systems are weak, students in crisis are more likely to be punished than helped.

THE ROLE OF SPECIAL EDUCATION AND DISABILITY SERVICES

Another important theme in the literature is the intersection between disability, incarceration, and school reentry. Youth in detention centers are significantly more likely to have undiagnosed or unaddressed learning disabilities, emotional disturbances, or mental health conditions.

Yet Individualized Education Programs (IEPs) often do not follow students into or out of custody. Teachers may be unaware of accommodations. Upon reentry, evaluations are rarely updated, and students are placed in general education classes without needed support.

This failure violates federal protections under the Individuals with Disabilities Education Act (IDEA), yet enforcement is inconsistent. As a result, students who qualify for special education services are disproportionately pushed out.

PROMISING PRACTICES IN REENTRY

While the landscape is bleak, the literature also points to promising models:

- **Transition Coordinators:** Staff who bridge communication between juvenile justice and schools have been shown to significantly increase re-enrollment and graduation rates (Bullis & Yovanoff, 2006).

- **Credit-bearing instruction in detention:** Programs that align curriculum with home districts and ensure transcripts follow the student show better outcomes.

- **Wraparound support:** Schools that provide integrated services, including mental health care, tutoring, and mentoring, create more stable reentry pathways.

- **Restorative practices:** Replacing punitive discipline with restorative justice helps reintegrate students into the school community.

These practices align with the components of the **FIRST Plan**, introduced later in this book. Unfortunately, implementation remains uneven, particularly in high-poverty, high-turnover districts.

FROM RETURN TO BELONGING

Reentry is more than a return; it is a reintroduction into a system that often never made room for the student in the first place. True reentry must move beyond paperwork, seat assignments, and vague encouragement. It must begin with the radical premise that formerly incarcerated youth are not a threat to manage but a future to invest in.

Reform efforts must prioritize four key shifts:

1. From Punishment to Partnership

Schools must abandon reactive, exclusionary policies and embrace restorative frameworks that repair harm without excluding students. Discipline should not be a barrier to belonging.

2. From Access to Engagement
    Merely enrolling students back into school is insufficient. They must be engaged, academically and emotionally, with instruction that meets them where they are, not where the system thinks they should be.

3. From Individual Blame to Systemic Responsibility
    Reentry is often framed as a student's second chance. However, is also the school system's second chance to show up differently, more humanely, than it did before. Reform means accountability at every level: school leadership, district policy, state funding, and teacher preparation.

4. From Isolation to Integration
    Formerly incarcerated students should not be siloed into alternative programs unless by choice and design. They deserve integration into the school community, with access to clubs, mentors, counselors, and leadership roles.

PROMISING PRACTICES IN THE FIELD

Across the country, a number of innovative programs have begun to model this kind of transformative reentry:

- The Oakland Unified School District developed a Juvenile Reentry Action Plan with assigned case managers and trauma-informed staff training for every returning student.

- The Center for Educational Excellence in Alternative Settings (CEEAS) supports facility-based schools in creating student-centered, project-based learning that is accredited and transferable.

- Restorative justice programs in places like Denver, Los Angeles, and Chicago have dramatically reduced recidivism and improved school climate by making community and accountability central.

A COLLECTIVE COMMITMENT

Reentry cannot rest solely on the shoulders of students or their families. It requires coordinated effort across systems ranging from schools, courts, community agencies to policymakers. This begins with a shift in mindset. These students do not return broken, they return with insight, resilience, and potential that has been tested under pressure.

As educators, advocates, and citizens, our task is not simply to let them back into schools, it is to make sure they feel like they belong.

CONCLUSION: DISCONNECTION AS A PREDICTABLE OUTCOME

Shania's experience of being told to "go downtown" instead of being welcomed back to her school isn't an anomaly. It's the predictable result of systems that were never designed for second chances.

This literature review reveals a stark truth: educational reentry for incarcerated youth is not a matter of chance, it's a matter of structure. Those structures, as they exist today, are failing.

To build an effective reentry system, we must redesign how schools view these students. Schools should not view these students as problems, but as young people deserving support, restoration, and opportunity.

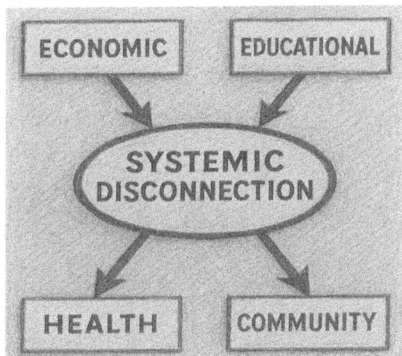

CHAPTER 3

Voices from the Ground
Study Methodology

"YOU GOTTA LISTEN TO THE PEOPLE WHO LIVE IT"

Mrs. Langston, a high school counselor with nearly twenty years of experience, sat across the table with her arms folded and her voice firm when she began speaking:

"If you're gonna study reentry, you better not leave out the people actually doing the reentry work. Teachers. Parents. Counselors. The students themselves. You gotta listen to the people who live it."

That sentiment became a compass for the research presented in this book. While statistics and policies offer a structural view of the issues surrounding reentry, it is the lived experience of those closest to the process that gives this work its most critical insights.

This chapter explains the methodology used to explore the perspectives of teachers, parents, and academic advisors who support formerly incarcerated youth transitioning back into high school. It also provides a rationale for centering the voices of those most impacted.

PURPOSE OF THE STUDY

The core aim of the study was to understand:

- The challenges formerly incarcerated students face when they reenter traditional school settings.

- The way teachers, parents, and academic advisors perceive and respond to those challenges.

- The support, strategies, and systems most effective in improving student outcomes.

This work was motivated by a rising dropout rate among formerly incarcerated students in one southern urban high school—Yellowtail High School (pseudonym). Between 2010 and 2017, students returning from juvenile detention centers dropped out at a disproportionately high rate. District leaders lacked qualitative insight into why this was happening or how to intervene effectively.

THEORETICAL FRAMEWORK: HIRSCHI'S SOCIAL CONTROL THEORY

This study was guided by **Hirschi's Social Control Theory** (1969), which posits that individuals with strong bonds to society, through family, school, and community, are less likely to engage in delinquent behavior. Hirschi identified four critical elements:

1. **Attachment** – emotional bonds with others.

2. **Commitment** – investment in conventional goals.

3. **Involvement** – participation in normative activities.

4. **Belief** – acceptance of moral validity of rules.

For youth reentering school, these bonds are often broken or fragile. The theory provided a lens for interpreting the ways schools, families, and support staff either reinforce or weaken these social ties.

RESEARCH DESIGN

This was a **qualitative descriptive study**, selected for its' ability to capture rich, detailed accounts of experience without imposing strict theoretical constraints. The study focused on gathering firsthand insights from those directly involved in the reentry process.

Semi-structured interviews were conducted with a total of **18 participants**:

- 6 teachers

- 6 parents or guardians

- 6 academic advisors

Participants were selected using purposeful sampling, ensuring they had recent experience with formerly incarcerated youth reentering Yellowtail High School.

SETTING AND PARTICIPANT DEMOGRAPHICS

The study took place in a mid-sized urban school district in the southern United States. Yellowtail High School serves approximately 1,200 students:

- 70% African American

- 25% Caucasian

- 5% Hispanic

The school had a documented dropout rate of 16%, well above the national average of 13% and below the county's 20%, according to Town Charts (2018). Among returning students from juvenile justice placements, the dropout rate was estimated to be as high as 35%.

Participants represented a cross-section of professional and personal experience:

- Teachers taught core academic subjects and special education.

- Advisors included school counselors and case managers.

- Parents included single mothers, grandparents, and foster guardians.

DATA COLLECTION

Interviews were conducted in person and over the phone, each lasting 30 to 60 minutes. Questions explored the following:

- Perceptions of student needs and behaviors.

- School climate and responsiveness.

- Available supports and service gaps.

- Suggestions for program or policy improvement.

All interviews were recorded (with consent), transcribed verbatim, and coded for themes using Hatch's (2002) nine-step typological analysis method.

DATA ANALYSIS

The analysis process followed these key steps:

1. **Identifying Typologies:** Categories such as "academic needs," "behavioral challenges," "staff training," "reentry support," and "family involvement."

2. **Coding the Data:** Interview transcripts were marked for statements aligning with each typology.

3. **Looking for Patterns:** Patterns were drawn across roles and perspectives.

4. **Determining Relationships:** Relationships among themes were examined—for example, how lack of staff training influenced perceptions of student behavior.

5. **Synthesizing Findings:** Core themes were developed and matched with recommendations.

To strengthen validity:

- Triangulation across participant roles was used.

- Member checks were offered, allowing participants to review key themes.

- Reflexive memos were kept throughout the process to monitor researcher bias.

LIMITATIONS

As with all qualitative work, this study does not claim generalizability. It is grounded in a specific context with a relatively small sample size. The insights, however, are transferable, particularly for other urban schools with similar student populations and systemic challenges.

EDUCATORS ON DISCIPLINE AND CULTURAL CHANGE

Teachers interviewed often described a sense of uncertainty around how to support formerly incarcerated students without compromising classroom norms.

"I want to be supportive," said Ms. Browning, a high school English teacher. "But when a student comes in with a history, the admin tells us to be careful. What does that even mean?"

Some educators admitted that training was either nonexistent or outdated.

"We had one Professional Development workshop about trauma-informed teaching," said a math teacher. "But it was mostly slides. No one told us what to do when a student shuts down or explodes."

Some educators expressed frustration with inconsistent messaging from leadership.

"One principal says give second chances. Another says write them up," shared Mr. Tran, a social studies teacher. "We're getting mixed messages, and the students can feel it."

A few teachers emphasized the potential of restorative practices but pointed out that true implementation requires more than a circle or a script.

"Restorative justice isn't just a meeting after a fight," said Ms. Cole, a guidance counselor. "It's how we treat students all the time." Ms. Cole continued, saying, "It's the difference between asking, 'What did you do?' and 'What happened to you?'"

In schools where trauma-informed training was integrated with staff collaboration, educators reported noticeable differences.

"When we met weekly as a team to talk about reentry students, it made all the difference," said Mr. Washington. "I learned about a student's home life, his triggers, and how to support him before things escalated."

Yet, these examples were the exception.

Many teachers felt caught between a punitive system and their own instincts for compassion.

"We're told to hold students accountable," one veteran teacher said, "but not taught how to do that in a way that doesn't break them."

This tension, between discipline and dignity, sits at the heart of school culture. Without a shared, intentional approach, schools risk perpetuating the same conditions that led students into the justice system in the first place.

Another limitation is that the student voice in this chapter is limited to second-hand perspectives. However, in **Chapter Nine**, the narratives of formerly incarcerated youth are centered directly, providing a powerful complement to the findings discussed here.

WHY THESE VOICES MATTER

The strength of this study lies in its focus on **people closest to the problem**, those who greet students on day one, sit with frustrated parents, and try to coax learning from a place of trauma and disruption.

"We see everything, but nobody ever asks us." one academic advisor shared.

This chapter offers a foundation. The chapters that follow build on the findings from these interviews to describe:

- The barriers students face (Chapter Four)

FAMILY PERSPECTIVES ON REENTRY BARRIERS

Parents and caregivers often carry the emotional and logistical weight of reentry alongside their children. Their voices reveal how systemic barriers extend beyond the school and into the home.

"He came home angry," said Mrs. Thompson, mother of a 10th-grade student who had been incarcerated for eight months. "Not at us, but at everything. He didn't trust anyone, not teachers, not counselors, not even his friends."

Several parents described feeling shut out of the school reentry process entirely.

"We got a letter saying he was being readmitted, but nobody met with us," said Mr. Alvarez, whose son had previously been placed in a detention center. "It was like, 'You figure it out.' But we didn't know what credits he had or what classes he needed."

The lack of mental health support was another recurring concern.

"I asked for a therapist when she came back," said one mother. "They said the school counselor could talk to her once a month. Once a month? After what she'd been through?"

Some families found themselves advocating for their children in systems they didn't fully understand.

"I didn't finish high school," said Ms. Greene. "So, when they started talking about transcripts and recovery plans, I nodded. But I didn't understand it. I just knew my son needed help."

These stories highlight the need for schools to partner with families, not just inform them, during the reentry process. When students return, their families return too, often without the support they need to rebuild trust, structure, and stability.

BEYOND THE OBVIOUS: OVERLOOKED BARRIERS TO REENTRY

While stigma, academic gaps, and behavioral expectations remain front-line challenges, many students return to school burdened by invisible obstacles that shape their daily experience and undermine their success.

CREDIT LOSS AND ACADEMIC DISRUPTION

Students often return from incarceration only to learn that the coursework completed during confinement doesn't count. Many juvenile facilities operate with minimal oversight or unaccredited programs.

"I passed my math class in there," said Antwan, 17. "But when I got back, they said it didn't count. That class was all I had."

This kind of credit loss not only delays graduation—it sends a message that their efforts while incarcerated were meaningless.

INCONSISTENT REENTRY PLANNING

Too often, students are also re-enrolled without any real plan. There's no meeting with staff, no review of mental health needs, and no one designated to follow up.

"He just showed up at the door," said one administrator. "We didn't even know he was coming back."

Without intentional transitions, reentry becomes a logistical task rather than a relational opportunity for restoration and support.

MENTAL HEALTH AND UNADDRESSED TRAUMA

Many returning students carry the weight of trauma, both from their incarceration and the environments that preceded it. Yet few schools offer immediate mental health screening upon reentry.

"I hadn't slept through the night in weeks, but they asked me what classes I wanted, not how I was doing," said Jasmine, (16).

Untreated trauma can manifest as withdrawal, aggression, apathy, or disassociation, none of which are well understood in punitive school cultures.

INSTABILITY AT HOME

Reentry is not just into school, it's into life. Some youth return to homes marked by economic stress, substance abuse, or unresolved family conflict.

"I was couch-surfing," said Deonte. "Nobody asked, they just told me to be on time."

This instability leads to attendance issues that are often met with punishment rather than inquiry.

LOSS OF POSITIVE PEER NETWORKS

Many students return to schools where former friends have moved on or worse, where old conflicts await. Some isolate themselves, others reengage with negative peer groups out of necessity.

"My old crew was still there," said Kareem. "That's who welcomed me back. I didn't want to get into trouble again, but they were the only ones who talked to me."

RECOGNIZING THE WHOLE PICTURE

These barriers are not as visible as a fight in the hallway or a missing homework assignment, but they are no less powerful. For reentry efforts to be effective, schools must look beneath the surface. This means asking new questions, offering new supports, and listening, really listening, to what students are saying with their behavior, silence, and resilience.

- What supports are most needed? (Chapter Five)

- A new framework for reentry success. (Chapter Six)

In their voices, we find not only problems but powerful solutions.

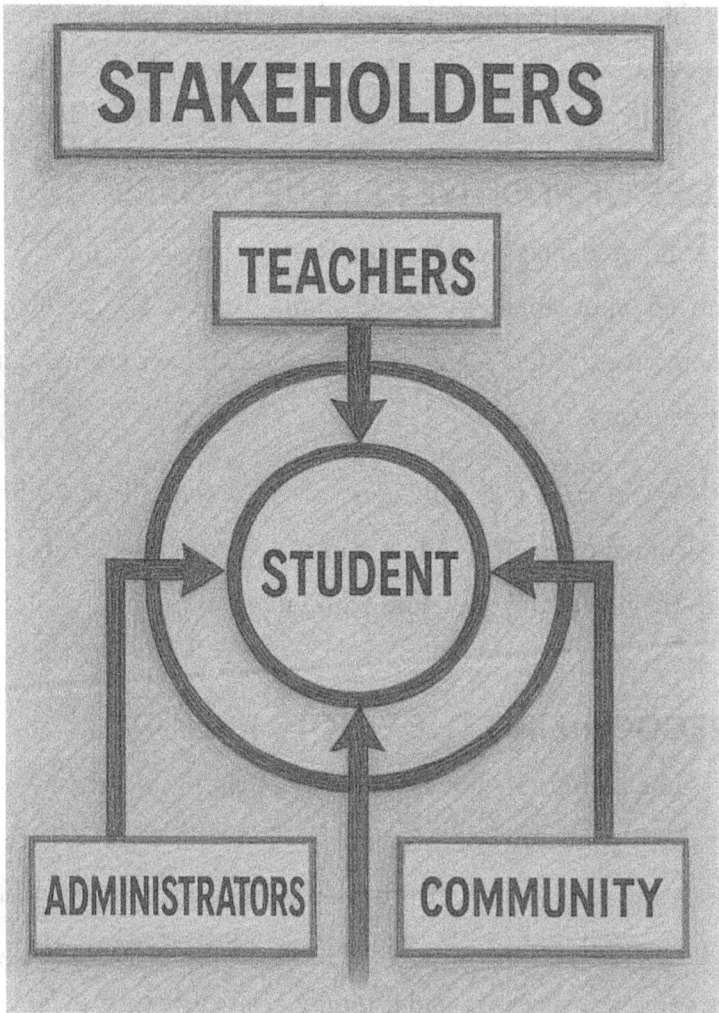

CHAPTER 4

Barriers to Reentry
Study Methodology

"THEY COME BACK, BUT THEY'RE ALREADY GONE"

Mr. Dalton, a high school history teacher with over a decade in the classroom, put it plainly during his interview:

> "They come back from juvie, but they're already gone. The system doesn't make room for them. It just lets them drift."

This haunting observation captures the essence of the problem. Formerly incarcerated students reenter public schools only to find that nothing has been prepared for them-not the curriculum, not the counseling, not the climate. They are technically present, but emotionally, academically, and socially disconnected.

This chapter explores the key barriers to reentry identified by teachers, parents, and academic advisors in the study. Their experiences shed light on why so many youths, like Jamal and Shania, fall through the cracks shortly after returning to school.

ACADEMIC DISENGAGEMENT AND CREDIT CONFUSION

The most frequently cited barrier was academic disengagement. Students often returned from incarceration with lost or unclear credits, placing them at a disadvantage that felt insurmountable.

"He thought he earned credits inside," one mother said of her son. "But when we brought the paperwork, the school said it didn't match their system. He had to repeat a whole semester."

Advisors echoed this frustration. Courses offered in detention centers often lacked alignment with state standards, and transcripts from juvenile facilities arrived late—if at all. This meant students reentered with no accurate academic record, making class placement guesswork at best.

For students already discouraged by their past experiences, repeating classes or being placed in remedial coursework only deepens their sense of failure.

BEHAVIORAL MISUNDERSTANDINGS AND MISTRUST

Many teachers described returning students as withdrawn or defiant, rarely both. Some came back angry, suspicious of authority, and quick to react. Others were silent, fearful of being judged or singled out.

Unfortunately, few schools offered reentry-specific behavioral supports. One teacher shared:

"We're told to treat them like any other student, but they're not. They just spent time in a locked facility. Some students are traumatized and some are scared. We're not trained to handle that."

Students are often met with zero-tolerance policies, even upon reentry. Minor infractions like being late, refusing to participate, and/or using cell phones can result in suspension or expulsion, reinforcing the cycle of exclusion.

STIGMA AND ISOLATION

Returning students frequently report feeling "watched," "judged," or "singled out." Word spreads quickly among peers. Some classmates are curious, others cruel. Educators may try to remain neutral, but unconscious bias creeps in.

"They look at me like I'm a criminal," said one student. "Not like someone trying to finish school."

A parent described the school staff's body language when her son returned:

"You could see it. They were nervous around him. Like he was going to snap."

This stigma is a quiet but powerful barrier. It isolates students from the school community and makes reintegration nearly impossible without intentional support.

MENTAL HEALTH AND TRAUMA

Teachers and advisors consistently pointed to unaddressed trauma as a root cause of many reentry struggles.

"One of my students came back after a fight in lock-up," said a school counselor. "He had a cut down his face and wouldn't talk to anyone. He just sat there. That wasn't defiance, that was trauma."

Yet most urban schools lack on-site mental health providers or trauma-informed care systems. Reentry meetings, if they happen at all, rarely include mental health professionals. Students are expected to self-regulate, even when they're still processing what happened during incarceration.

Parents feel this gap deeply. One mother said:

"He came back angry and scared. But nobody at school asked about that. They just asked if he had his schedule."

FAMILY STRAIN AND LACK OF SUPPORT

Many students reenter school while also navigating unstable home environments like poverty, homelessness, family conflict, or the threat of returning to court supervision.

Advisors noted that parents often feel overwhelmed:

- They don't know how to advocate for services.

- They fear judgment from school staff.

- They are managing multiple responsibilities, including other children, employment, or their own legal issues.

"We needed help," one parent explained. "But they made me feel like it was my fault."

Schools often fail to engage families meaningfully in the reentry process. There is no protocol for family meetings, no checklist of reentry supports, no single point of contact. As one advisor put it:

"It's like everybody is guessing. The family is guessing, the school is guessing, but the kid is paying the price."

LACK OF A COORDINATED PLAN

Perhaps the most significant barrier, repeated by nearly every participant, was the **lack of a structured reentry plan**. No designated staff member. No orientation. No academic review. No individualized schedule. Students simply showed up and were placed into the system without ceremony or support.

"We just plug them back in like they were never gone," said one advisor. "But they were gone, and a lot happened while they were gone."

This institutional amnesia, pretending nothing happened, prevents healing, accountability, or planning. It leaves students to navigate reentry alone, often setting them up for failure.

SYSTEMIC INEQUITIES

Finally, participants acknowledged that these barriers do not exist in a vacuum. They are compounded by larger structural inequities:

- Underfunded urban schools
- High teacher turnover
- Over-policed campuses
- Racial disparities in discipline
- Insufficient special education supports

Reentry challenges are not just the result of individual behaviors or isolated gaps; they are the product of systems designed without these students in mind.

CONCLUSION: SEEN, BUT UNSUPPORTED

Formerly incarcerated students return to school with the hope of a fresh start. But instead of finding a bridge, they encounter a wall built from stigma, disorganization, and systemic neglect.

This chapter has presented the key barriers these students face from the perspective of those who know them best: their teachers, their families, and their advisors.

In the next chapter, we shift from barriers to **possibilities**. Drawing from these same voices, we explore what supports are most needed and most effective in helping students not only return but thrive.

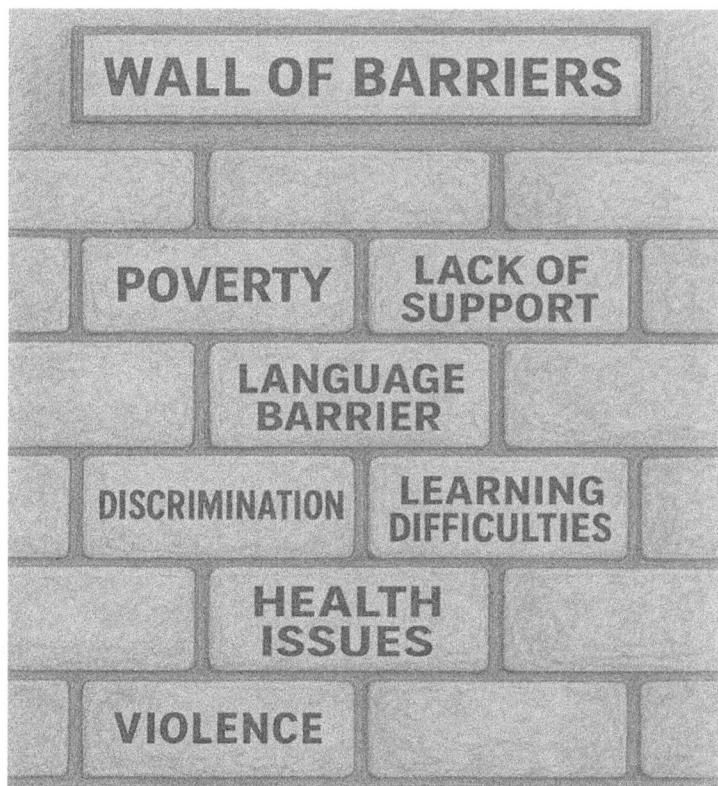

WALL OF BARRIERS

POVERTY   LACK OF SUPPORT

LANGUAGE BARRIER

DISCRIMINATION   LEARNING DIFFICULTIES

HEALTH ISSUES

VIOLENCE

CHAPTER 5

What They Need
Supports, Services, and Recommendations

"HE NEEDED A BRIDGE, NOT A TEST"

Ms. Ayala, an academic advisor at Yellowtail High School, remembered a student named Tyrell who returned from juvenile detention after eight months.

"He came in with one bag and no transcript. First day back, they gave him a schedule and a benchmark test. He sat down, looked at the paper, and just froze. He needed a bridge, not a test."

Tyrell's story illustrates a common mistake schools make, expecting reentering students to assimilate immediately into the academic routine, without addressing the emotional, structural, or instructional needs created by months of disruption. Instead of scaffolding support, we too often measure performance.

This chapter focuses on what students like Tyrell need to succeed. We will discuss what educators, parents, and advisors identified as the most critical supports for effective reentry. These findings directly informed the development of the **FIRST Plan** in the following chapter.

A WARM WELCOME

One of the most basic yet powerful recommendations was the idea of a **structured**, **welcoming** reentry process.

"When they walk in the door, there should be someone waiting," said a parent. "Someone who knows where they've been and what they've been through."

Advisors and teachers stressed the value of an orientation session, a welcome-back meeting with a counselor, and a check-in with someone who could help the student build a schedule that made sense.

"Even just knowing someone expects them, and has a plan can change everything," one counselor explained.

REENTRY CASE MANAGERS OR COORDINATORS

Several participants proposed the creation of a dedicated **reentry coordinator or case manager** role. This person would:

- Communicate with the juvenile facility before release

- Gather and review academic records

- Set up a reentry meeting with teachers, parents, and the student

- Monitor academic progress for the first 90 days

"Right now, nobody owns the reentry process," said one advisor. "If there was one person in charge, we'd stop losing kids in the cracks."

This model aligns with best practices in reentry programs nationwide, where continuity and accountability are key to success.

CREDIT TRANSFER AND FLEXIBLE SCHEDULING

Academic frustration was a recurring theme in earlier chapters, and the solutions were equally clear: students need accurate **credit assessments** and **flexible scheduling options**.

Advisors recommended:

- Immediate transcript evaluation upon reentry

- Partnerships with juvenile facilities to align curriculum and credit policies

- Online or night school options to recover lost credits without grade-level penalties

"They want to graduate, but they feel so far behind," one advisor said. "We need to give them real pathways to catch up."

One teacher added that flexible scheduling could also mean allowing part-time reentry, modified course loads, or hybrid learning to ease the transition back into a full school day.

TRAUMA-INFORMED MENTAL HEALTH SUPPORT

Every participant emphasized the need for **on-site, accessible mental health support** for reentering students.

"These kids have seen things we don't talk about in schools," said a teacher. "And we expect them to just pick up a pencil like everything's fine?"

Recommendations included:

- Daily or weekly check-ins with school counselors or psychologists

- Group counseling sessions for reentering students

- Partnerships with local mental health agencies for wraparound services

Parents especially voiced a desire for **trauma-informed care** staff trained to understand the emotional impact of incarceration and capable of responding with empathy rather than discipline.

MENTORSHIP AND PEER SUPPORT

Many students come back from detention centers feeling isolated or ashamed. One of the most promising solutions cited was **mentorship**.

"He had no one to talk to. He needed someone who'd been there," a teacher said of a returning student.

Several participants recommended peer mentoring programs or alumni networks linking formerly incarcerated students with older youth or adults who had successfully navigated the reentry process.

Such mentors could:

- Provide hope and perspective
- Help with goal setting
- Serve as a buffer between students and the school's impersonal bureaucracy

One advisor suggested a weekly "Reentry Circle." This would be a safe space for students to talk, problem-solve, and support each other.

RESTORATIVE JUSTICE PRACTICES

Some of the most powerful insights came from teachers who had experience with **restorative justice**.

Instead of punishing students for misbehavior, these practices focus on relationship-building, accountability, and healing.

"We had a circle with a student who got into a fight," said one teacher. "He talked about what it felt like being locked up. Other kids listened, really listened. That was the first time I saw him smile since he came back."

Participants recommended:

- Training all staff in restorative approaches
- Incorporating circles or conferences into disciplinary policies
- Using restorative practices proactively as part of reentry, not just reactively

INCREASED FAMILY ENGAGEMENT

Parents and guardians felt left out of the reentry process. Schools, they said, often failed to communicate consistently or respectfully.

"They wait until something goes wrong," said one mother. "Then they call me. But I never get a call to ask how he's doing or what he needs."

Recommendations included:

- Reentry planning meetings that include families

- Regular progress updates through phone calls, texts, or home visits

- Parent liaisons or advocates who can help families navigate school systems

Strengthening the **home-school partnership** was seen as essential for sustaining student motivation and accountability.

STAFF TRAINING AND CULTURAL COMPETENCE

Educators acknowledged a training gap.

"We weren't taught how to work with youth coming out of incarceration," one teacher admitted. "I had to figure it out through trial and error."

Participants called for professional development that includes:

- Trauma-informed practices

- De-escalation strategies

- Cultural humility

- Understanding juvenile justice processes

This training would not only improve outcomes for returning students but also reduce teacher burnout and improve school climate.

SAFE, SUPPORTIVE SCHOOL ENVIRONMENTS

Finally, students need to feel safe. Students need to feel safe not just physically, but also emotionally. That means schools must move from punitive environments to **supportive ones**.

Recommendations included:

- Fewer school police, more counselors

- Positive behavior supports

- Clear anti-stigma messaging for students returning from detention centers

"Let them come back with dignity," said one advisor. "Let them know they're still part of this community."

CONCLUSION: FROM SURVIVAL TO SUCCESS

What formerly incarcerated students need is not mysterious. The stakeholders closest to them have been calling for these supports for years.

This chapter has outlined a clear set of services, practices, and system changes. These changes range from case management and mental health to mentorship and family engagement. These things can help students not only survive reentry but succeed in school and life.

In the next chapter, these insights come together in a unified, research-informed model: the **FIRST Plan**, a framework for reentry success designed specifically for urban high schools like Yellowtail.

CHAPTER 6

The FIRST Plan
A Framework for
Reentry Success

"WE NEEDED A PLAN, NOT A PATCH"

After nearly a decade working as a school administrator, Dr. L. Thomas watched the same story unfold year after year: a student returned from juvenile detention, walked into the front office, and was placed into classes without so much as a conversation. The school would scramble to locate records, teachers would complain they weren't informed, and within weeks, sometimes days, the student would disengage.

"We weren't building a bridge, we were handing kids duct tape and saying, 'Patch it up yourself!'" said Dr. Thomas.

This chapter presents the **FIRST Plan**, a comprehensive reentry framework designed to provide structure, support, and sustainability for youth returning to school after incarceration. It emerged from the data collected during this study and reflects the lived realities of educators, advisors, families, and students.

WHY THE FIRST PLAN?

Too often, reentry strategies are reactive and fragmented. There is no designated process, no person accountable, and no consistent plan for academic and emotional support. The result is predictable: students fall through the cracks.

The FIRST Plan provides a **proactive, school-centered framework** for reentry, guided by five core values:

- Focus on Collaboration

- Integrated Mental Health Services

- Remediation and Tutoring

- Supportive Mentorship and Counseling

- Transitional Alternatives and Community Engagement

Together, these components address the academic, social, emotional, and systemic challenges that returning youth face.

F – Focus on Collaboration Between Educational and Juvenile Justice Systems

WHAT IT LOOKS LIKE:

- Ongoing communication between juvenile detention centers and school districts

- Shared academic records and behavior reports

- Pre-release planning involving counselors and administrators

WHY IT MATTERS

Youth returning from detention centers often do so with little coordination between agencies. Teachers and staff are left uninformed. The student is left to self-advocate in a system that has historically marginalized them.

A coordinated approach ensures:

- Proper credit transfer

- Accurate class placement

- Continuity of special education and support services

"If I'd known what he was doing in detention, I could've helped him pick up where he left off," one math teacher noted.

I – Integrated Onsite Mental Health Services

WHAT IT LOOKS LIKE:

- Mental health counselors embedded in the school building

- Trauma-informed training for staff

- Routine wellness check-ins for returning students

WHY IT MATTERS

Students return from incarceration carrying deep trauma, often unspoken and unacknowledged. Without mental health support, that trauma surfaces as absenteeism, classroom disruption, or withdrawal.

Integrated services provide:

- Early intervention

- Emotional regulation support

- A safe outlet for processing reentry challenges

"He had panic attacks in the hallway," a parent shared. "Not because he was bad, but because he was scared. Therapy helped."

R – Remediation and Tutoring

WHAT IT LOOKS LIKE:

- Individualized learning plans based on reentry assessment

- Access to tutoring during and after school

- Summer programs for credit recovery

WHY IT MATTERS

Reentry students often reenter school significantly behind their peers. Standard pacing and rigid graduation timelines can feel insurmountable.

Targeted remediation helps students:

- Catch up academically without stigma

- Gain confidence in core subjects

- Prepare for graduation or GED pathways

"He didn't need an easier class," one advisor said. "He needed someone to sit with him and say, 'You're not dumb, you just missed some steps.'"

S – Supportive Mentorship and Counseling

WHAT IT LOOKS LIKE:

- Peer mentors who have successfully completed reentry

- Assigned adult mentors (e.g., teachers, staff, community volunteers)

- Group sessions focused on life skills, career planning, and emotional resilience

WHY IT MATTERS

Reentering students often lack a stable adult relationship in the school building. They need someone to believe in them and to walk with them.

Mentorship provides:

- Belonging and emotional safety

- Guidance through difficult transitions

- A buffer against stigma and isolation

"She met with her mentor every week," a teacher explained. "And for the first time, she had someone who wasn't judging her, just listening."

T – Transitional Alternatives and Community Engagement

WHAT IT LOOKS LIKE:

- Part-time or hybrid schedules for transitional students

- Connections to job training, apprenticeships, or dual enrollment

- Community partnerships for housing, food security, and legal aid

WHY IT MATTERS

Not every student can or should return full-time immediately. Life outside school, court appointments, family obligations, and /or trauma recovery can make traditional schedules unworkable.

Transitional alternatives:

- Honor students' real-life responsibilities

- Prevent dropouts by adapting to context

- Extend learning beyond the classroom

"We set up a work-study program through a local nonprofit," said one administrator. "He started showing up to school just so he could stay in that program."

PUTTING IT ALL TOGETHER

The FIRST Plan is not just a checklist; it is a **mindset**. It asks educators, administrators, and policymakers to treat reentry not as a formality but as a sacred responsibility. These students have already been failed once. Schools must not fail them again.

Implementation requires:

- Leadership buy-in

- Designated staff roles

- Ongoing training

- Partnerships with families and community organizations

It also requires compassion, patience, and a commitment to equity.

CONCLUSION: FROM FRAMEWORK TO REALITY

"It's not about fixing kids," Dr. Thomas said. "It's about fixing the systems around them."

The FIRST Plan offers a blueprint for schools that want to become places of restoration, not re-traumatization. It builds on the real needs identified by those doing the work every day.

In the next chapters, we explore how this framework can be aligned with policy, infused into school culture, and sustained over time.

FIRST PLAN

Family Engagement · Reentry Planning · Skilled Training · Transition Programs · Incentivized Participation · Individual Assessment

CHAPTER 7

Policy and Practice
Aligning Systems for Reentry Support

"WE CAN'T KEEP DOING THIS PIECEMEAL"

In a tense school board meeting, a community advocate stood to speak. She was the guardian of a 17-year-old who had returned from juvenile detention six weeks earlier and was already on the verge of dropping out again.

"There's no system," she said. "No checklist. No reentry team. No accountability. We can't keep doing this piecemeal. These kids deserve a coordinated plan."

Her frustration is widely shared. Across the country, well-intentioned efforts to support formerly incarcerated youth are hampered by a lack of alignment between policy and practice. This chapter examines the policy landscape that shapes reentry efforts and offers concrete strategies for better alignment.

THE POLICY GAP

At the federal, state, and local levels, there is growing recognition of the need to support youth reentry. However, **policy guidance is often vague, underfunded, or poorly enforced.**

Key Challenges:

- **Fragmented governance:** Juvenile justice systems operate separately from public education systems.

- **Lack of mandates:** Few states require schools to accept reentering students unconditionally—or to provide transitional support.

- **Inconsistent enforcement:** Laws like IDEA and McKinney-Vento are not always implemented for students returning from incarceration.

- **Insufficient funding:** Schools receive no additional funds for reentry services unless they secure grants or reallocate existing resources.

"We talk about reentry like it's a priority," one district leader shared. "But we don't resource it like one."

RELEVANT FEDERAL POLICIES

Several federal laws intersect with youth reentry, though none were designed specifically for it.

1. **Individuals with Disabilities Education Act (IDEA)**

   - Mandates special education services for eligible students, including during incarceration.

   - Requires schools to maintain continuity of services.

   - Common gap: IEPs often do not follow students back to school.

2. **Every Student Succeeds Act (ESSA)**

   - Encourages educational stability for at-risk youth.

   - Requires states to report disaggregated discipline and graduation data.

   - Common gap: No explicit mandates around reentry planning or support services.

3. **McKinney-Vento Homeless Assistance Act**

   - Protects students experiencing housing instability, often relevant for youth returning from detention.

   - Common gap: Schools may not identify reentering youth as eligible, missing key services.

These policies provide a legal foundation but lack specificity and enforcement mechanisms when applied to reentry.

STATE AND LOCAL POLICY TRENDS

Some states have taken proactive steps:

- **California:** Requires educational liaisons in juvenile courts and mandates that schools accept returning students within three days of release.

- **Texas:** Allows for the creation of reentry transition plans in Individual Graduation Committees.

- **Illinois:** Offers reentry grants to districts that serve high numbers of returning youth.

However, in many places—including the southern urban district at the center of this study—**policy varies from district to district.** Most schools lack reentry protocols, and decisions are made ad hoc.

SCHOOL-LEVEL PRACTICES THAT WORK

Even in the absence of strong policy, some schools have pioneered effective practices. These align closely with the FIRST Plan and include:

- **Dedicated reentry teams:** A multidisciplinary team (counselor, administrator, teacher, mentor) assigned to each returning student.

- **Reentry intake meetings:** Held within 72 hours of reentry to assess needs and develop a plan.

- **Memoranda of Understanding (MOUs):** Agreements between juvenile justice agencies and schools for data sharing and continuity of services.

- **Professional development:** Required training for staff on trauma-informed practices and the reentry process.

"We wrote our own protocol," one principal shared. "It's not perfect, but it's better than waiting for the state to tell us what to do."

RECOMMENDATIONS FOR POLICY ALIGNMENT

To bridge the gap between policy and practice, this study offers several recommendations:

1. **Mandate Reentry Protocols**

   - States should require school districts to develop reentry procedures, including intake meetings, mental health screenings, and credit evaluations.

2. **Fund Reentry Roles**

   - Allocate funding for reentry coordinators, transition specialists, or case managers in schools with high reentry populations.

3. **Standardize Credit Transfers**

   - Create statewide agreements for credit reciprocity between detention centers and home schools.

4. **Enforce Special Education Compliance**
    *   Monitor and enforce IDEA protections for incarcerated and returning students, especially regarding IEP updates and implementation.

5. **Collect and Report Reentry Data**
    *   Require schools to track enrollment, attendance, achievement, and graduation rates of formerly incarcerated students.

6. **Foster Interagency Collaboration**
    *   State and local governments should convene cross-system councils to align juvenile justice, education, child welfare, and mental health systems.

A VISION FOR SYSTEMIC CHANGE

Policy must evolve from a passive backdrop to an active driver of support. This means shifting from:

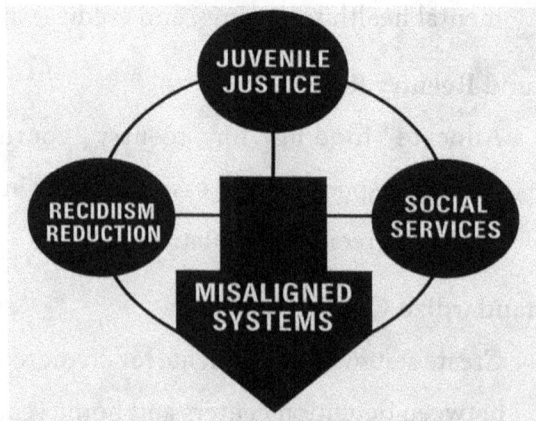

- *Compliance* to **care**

- *Isolation* to **integration**

- *Punishment* to **preparation**

Reentry support is not just about welcoming a student back into a building, it's about welcoming them back into a future.

CONCLUSION: MOVING FROM POLICY TO PRACTICE

"Policy is the promise," said one superintendent. "Practice is the delivery."

If schools are to fulfill their promise to every child, regardless of past mistakes, they must be equipped with the right policies, resources, and mindsets. Aligning systems for reentry is not only a matter of equity. It is a matter of justice.

In the next chapter, we shift from policy to practice on the ground, exploring how educator training and school culture shape the daily experience of reentering students.

CHAPTER 8

Educator Training and School Culture

"YOU CAN'T TEACH WHAT YOU DON'T UNDERSTAND"

Mr. Benton, a veteran English teacher at Yellowtail High, recalled the moment one of his students returned from juvenile detention. The boy, once expressive and eager, now sat in silence, staring at his desk for days. Benton tried everything: praise, pressure, patience. Nothing worked.

"I didn't know what he'd been through and I didn't know what to do," Benton admitted. "You can't teach what you don't understand."

That moment of confusion, frustration, and missed connection captures a central challenge in reentry work: most educators care, but they are unprepared.

This chapter explores the critical role that teacher and staff training plays in creating a reentry-ready school culture. Without a shared understanding, without the tools to respond to trauma and disconnection, even the best intentions can fall short.

THE CULTURE OF THE BUILDING MATTERS

Schools are more than buildings, they are ecosystems. Within these systems, **culture is everything**. When the school culture is hostile, rigid, or punitive, reentering students sense it immediately. When it is inclusive, flexible, and restorative, they have a chance to thrive.

"If the vibe is that they're criminals, they won't stay," said one school counselor. "But if the vibe is, 'We're glad you're back,' they might."

Participants across roles—teachers, parents, and advisors—stressed that **what happens in the classroom** is just as important as what happens in policy meetings. School culture is shaped not only by what we say, but by what we model.

PROFESSIONAL DEVELOPMENT: WHAT EDUCATORS NEED

The data revealed five key training areas educators need to effectively support formerly incarcerated students:

1. **Trauma-Informed Practices**
    Many returning students have experienced physical violence, emotional neglect, instability, or isolation.

Trauma-informed educators recognize that challenging behavior may be a **symptom of survival**, not defiance.

"I learned to stop asking, 'What's wrong with you?' and start asking, 'What happened to you?'" said a teacher who had undergone trauma training.

Training should include:

- Recognizing trauma responses (e.g., shutdowns, outbursts)

- De-escalation techniques

- Creating predictable and safe learning environments

2. **Decriminalizing Language and Expectations**
   Educators must examine how their own language, tone, and assumptions can reinforce stigma.

"We used to call them 'the jail kids,'" one staff member confessed. "We didn't mean harm, but it showed how we saw them."

Training should address:

- Implicit bias and deficit framing

- Restorative language and affirming communication

- Holding high expectations without shaming

3. **Reentry Procedures and Policies**
   Many teachers reported feeling **uninformed** when a student returned from detention centers. They didn't know the student's background, needs, or status.

"I found out from a kid in class," said one teacher. "Nobody told me. I felt unprepared and honestly a little nervous."

Training should ensure all staff know:

- How reentry works in their district

- Who the point-of-contact is

- What supports the student has or needs

4. **Special Education and Legal Rights**
   Several students returning from detention centers have IEPs or qualify for accommodations. Teachers must know:

- How to access and implement IEPs

- What legal protections apply under IDEA

- Who to contact for help

Failure to implement accommodations can lead to legal violations and educational harm.

5. **Culturally Responsive and Equity-Based Teaching**
   Youth of color, particularly Black and Latinx youth, are disproportionately impacted by school pushout and incarceration. Educators must be

equipped to teach with cultural humility and a justice-oriented mindset.

"We're not just teaching content," one teacher reflected. "We're teaching students who've survived systems."

Training in equity includes:

- Understanding systemic racism and its impact on education

- Incorporating diverse voices and histories into the curriculum

- Building relationships rooted in respect and trust

BUILDING REENTRY-READY CLASSROOMS

A reentry-ready classroom is one where students feel **seen, safe, and supported.** Teachers who successfully reintegrate students often share certain strategies:

- Greet returning students with warmth, not interrogation.

- Offer flexibility in assignments while maintaining high standards.

- Build connections before focusing on content.

- Use restorative check-ins to understand what students are carrying emotionally.

- Create small wins to rebuild confidence.

"When I saw she passed her first quiz back, I celebrated it out loud," said one teacher. "It reminded her that she could still succeed here."

LEADERSHIP AND CULTURE CHANGE

School leaders play a crucial role in setting the tone. Principals who prioritize reentry create a ripple effect:

- They allocate time for training

- They protect the dignity of returning students

- They model empathy and accountability for staff

One principal described starting every faculty meeting with a "student spotlight":

"We focus on a reentry student each month, not their record, but their progress. It reminds us why we do this work."

Changing culture doesn't happen overnight, but it begins with naming the values: restoration over retribution, belonging over behavior control and relationship over rigidity.

BARRIERS TO IMPLEMENTATION

Despite enthusiasm, educators reported barriers:

- Time: Full schedules leave little room for training or mentorship.

- Turnover: Staff changes disrupt continuity.

- Fear: Lack of experience with justice-involved youth creates hesitation.

- Systemic pressure: High stakes testing and rigid curricula limit flexibility.

Addressing these barriers requires systemic support from districts, unions, and state policy.

CONCLUSION: TEACHING AS RESTORATION

"Reentry isn't just a process, it's a pedagogy," said a curriculum specialist. "It's how we teach, how we see our students, and how we hold hope for them."

This chapter has outlined the training, strategies, and cultural shifts needed to support formerly incarcerated students not just academically, but humanely.

In the next chapter, the spotlight shifts to the youth themselves. Their voices—raw, reflective, and resilient— offer the most important insight of all.

CHAPTER 9

Student Voices
Reflections and Realities

"THEY DON'T SEE THE WHOLE ME"

During a quiet moment in a school counselor's office, seventeen-year-old Malik summed up his experience with a sentence that lingers long after the interview ended:

"They see my file, not my face. They don't see the whole me."

Malik's insight speaks to the heart of the reentry crisis, not just as a matter of academics or behavior, but as an identity struggle. This chapter centers the voices of formerly incarcerated students themselves, weaving together their reflections, fears, dreams, and truths.

Their stories add depth and urgency to the research and recommendations in previous chapters. They remind us that behind every policy, protocol, or program is a person— young, complex, and deserving of more than survival.

JAMAL – "NO ONE ASKED WHAT I NEEDED"

Jamal's journey began in middle school with suspensions for minor behavior such as talking back and skipping class. By age fifteen, he was sent to a juvenile facility after a fight escalated on school property.

"It was quick," he recalled. "One day I was in class, the next I was in court."

Inside the facility, education felt disjointed. Jamal said the teachers meant well, but "the work didn't count." When he returned to Yellowtail High, he found himself placed back in the same courses he had already failed.

"No one asked what I needed. They just gave me a schedule."

He lasted two months before dropping out. Now working at a fast-food restaurant, he said he still thinks about returning to school but doesn't know how.

SHANIA – "I HAD TO PRETEND I WAS OKAY"

Shania's incarceration followed a shoplifting charge at age sixteen. She spent five months in a detention center and returned home determined to finish high school.

"I had a plan," she said. "But when I got back, everything felt... off."

She described teachers avoiding eye contact, students whispering, and counselors treating her "like a case file." There was no reentry meeting, no mental health check-in and no flexibility when she fell behind on assignments.

"I had to pretend I was okay just to stay in school."

By her second semester, her grades had slipped, and she was skipping classes to avoid questions. A peer mentor, another student who had returned from detention, was the only person she trusted.

"He got it," she said. "He didn't ask for details. He just sat with me at lunch."

Shania eventually graduated—barely—but said the experience left scars. "They let me finish," she said. "But I didn't feel like I belonged."

DARIUS – "I WAS TRYING TO CHANGE, BUT THEY KEPT LOOKING AT WHO I WAS"

Darius was sixteen when he returned from juvenile detention, having served nearly a year for a probation violation. When he reentered Yellowtail High, he was placed in crowded classes, often with younger students.

"They didn't care that I was trying to change," he said. "They kept looking at who I was."

He described constant surveillance from staff, random locker checks, and being referred to the office for "attitude" when he questioned assignments. Despite this, Darius passed his classes—thanks, he said, to a history teacher who gave him extra time and checked in regularly.

"She didn't treat me like I was broken," he said. "She just asked me what I needed to get the work done."

Darius now attends a community college. He wants to be a probation officer, "one who actually listens."

AALIYAH – "SCHOOL WAS THE EASY PART. LIFE WAS THE HARD PART."

Aaliyah returned to school after eight months in a youth facility. Her biggest challenge wasn't grades; it was everything else.

"My mom was gone. I had to take care of my little brother. I was couch surfing. School was the easy part; life was the hard part."

Despite these obstacles, Aaliyah showed up every day, tired but determined. She credits her success to a counselor who created a flexible schedule and found her a mentor through a local nonprofit.

"She didn't fix everything," Aaliyah said. "But she made sure I wasn't alone."

Aaliyah graduated at nineteen. She now works at a reentry center helping other young women adjust to life after incarceration.

THEMES FROM STUDENT NARRATIVES

From these and other stories, several key themes emerged:

1. **Lack of Recognition**

    Students returned to schools where no one acknowledged their absence or their growth. The silence was often more painful than judgment.

2. **Stigma and Surveillance**

    Many students felt watched, not welcomed. They reported being treated differently, disciplined faster, and trusted less than their peers.3. **The Power of One Caring Adult**

    In nearly every story, one person, teacher, counselor and/or mentor made the difference between disengagement and persistence.

4. **Emotional Labor**

    Students carried emotional burdens: shame, anxiety, trauma, pressure to support family. Few received mental health support.

5. **Need for Belonging**

What students wanted most wasn't pity, it was a sense of belonging. A sense that they were more than their past, that they had a place and a future.

STUDENT RECOMMENDATIONS

When asked what schools should do differently, students were clear:

"I felt like I didn't belong."	"No one understood what I was going through."	"I didn't have anyone who cared."	"I want to make a better life for myself.
– Student	– Student	– Student	– Student

- "Have a real meeting when we come back. Not just a schedule."

- "Train teachers to understand what we've been through."

- "Give us someone we can talk to who's not judging us."

- "Make sure our credits count."

- "Don't let us feel invisible."

CONCLUSION: TRUTH FROM THE SOURCE

This chapter has presented not just data, but truth from the mouths of those most affected. Student voices are not sidebars to reentry work; they are its moral compass.

"If they'd just asked me what I needed," Malik said again before leaving the interview, "I might've stayed."

Their stories fuel the urgency behind reentry reform. In the final chapter, we turn to what comes next: how to sustain this work, scale it, and reimagine school systems that no longer push students out, but pull them back in.

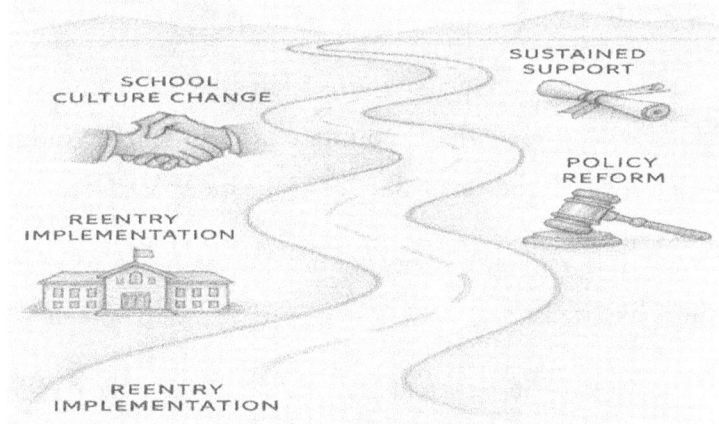

THE ROAD AHEAD

SUSTAINED SUPPORT

SCHOOL CULTURE CHANGE

POLICY REFORM

REENTRY IMPLEMENTATION

REENTRY IMPLEMENTATION

REFLECTIONS ON GROWTH AND HOPE

The students interviewed for this study did not speak only of struggle; they also expressed growth, self-awareness, and a desire for something more.

"When I got out, I promised myself I wouldn't go back," said Jamari, 18. "But school didn't feel any different. The same teachers, the same looks. I had to be different, so I kept my head down and just kept moving."

Others described the tension between wanting to succeed and feeling unsupported.

"They tell you to stay on track, but no one checks if the track's even there," said Kenya, who returned to school after six months in a detention center. "I want to graduate. I just wish it didn't feel like I'm doing it alone."

Some students reconnected with education in unexpected ways.

"Art was the only class where I felt like a person," said DeShawn. "I drew what I couldn't say. My teacher didn't ask a bunch of questions. She just gave me space."

Many still held onto hope, not just for themselves, but for others like them.

"They need to hear us," said Malaya. "We're not broken. We're trying. We just need someone to see us and not our record."

These student voices do more than highlight barriers they offer a vision for what school could be if designed with dignity, trust, and humanity at the center.

CHAPTER 10

The Road Ahead
Sustainability, Scale, and Future Research

"WE CAN'T AFFORD TO TREAT THIS LIKE A PILOT"

At the conclusion of a community roundtable on youth reentry, a local nonprofit leader stood up and addressed the crowd:

"We've been treating reentry like a pilot program, something temporary, something optional. But this isn't a pilot, it's a crisis. We can't afford to treat it like anything less than permanent, systemic work."

Her words captured the challenge ahead. This book has laid out the problems facing formerly incarcerated youth returning to urban high schools: academic loss, trauma, stigma, disconnection, and a lack of coordinated support. It has also offered a framework—the **FIRST Plan**—grounded in the voices of students, educators, and families. However, none of it matters if schools can't sustain it, scale it, and build on it over time.

This final chapter explores what it takes to move from isolated success stories to **system-wide transformation.**

SUSTAINING REENTRY WORK: MAKING IT LAST

Short-term initiatives often fade because they rely on:

- One passionate individual

- Temporary grant funding

- Crisis-driven urgency

Sustainability means embedding reentry into the core mission of schools, not the margins.

Keys to Sustainability:

1. **Leadership Commitment**
   - Principals and superintendents must champion reentry as a priority.

   - Policies must be written, funded, and enforced, not left to personal discretion.

2. **Dedicated Roles**
   - Schools should create permanent positions like *Reentry Coordinators, Transition Specialists,* or *Wraparound Counselors.*

3. **Budget Alignment**

- Districts must allocate stable funding, not rely solely on outside grants.

- Title I, IDEA, and mental health dollars can often be braided to support FIRST Plan components.

4. **Ongoing Training**
   - Reentry training must be part of induction, PD calendars, and school improvement plans.

   - Trauma-informed and culturally responsive pedagogy should become standard, not supplemental.

5. **Family and Community Partnerships**
   - Sustaining success means schools don't act alone. Community organizations, mental health agencies, and youth advocates must be partners at the table.

"If it's not in the school's DNA, it won't survive a principal change," one advisor warned. "It has to be built in."

SCALING THE FIRST PLAN: FROM ONE SCHOOL TO MANY

The FIRST Plan was designed with flexibility in mind. While its components are grounded in the experiences of one southern urban high school, its framework can be adapted and scaled across districts.

Steps to Scale:

1. **Assess Local Needs**
   - Use school data to identify students with a history of incarceration.
   - Map existing supports and service gaps.

2. **Start Small, Build Big**
   - Pilot FIRST with a targeted group, refine the approach, and then expand district wide.
   - Begin with one or two components like mentorship or trauma-informed training and scale incrementally.

3. **Develop Toolkits and Protocols**
   - Create clear reentry intake forms, meeting templates, tracking tools, and checklists that schools can implement with fidelity.

4. **Form Interagency Coalitions**
   - Bring juvenile justice, education, social services, and community partners into regular coordination meetings.

5. **Share Success Stories**
   - Highlight wins—graduations, successful transitions, reduced recidivism. Stories create momentum and buy-in.

6. **Evaluate and Adjust**

- Use both quantitative and qualitative data to monitor outcomes.

- Be responsive to feedback from students, families, and frontline staff.

"We don't need a cookie-cutter approach," said one superintendent. "We need a common framework with local flavor."

FUTURE RESEARCH: QUESTIONS STILL TO ANSWER

While this study offers valuable insights, many questions remain unanswered. Future research should explore:

1. **Long-Term Outcomes**
   - How do formerly incarcerated students fare 1, 3, or 5 years after reentry?
   - What factors predict persistence in school versus dropout or recidivism?

2. **Student Identity and Resilience**
   - How do students reconstruct identity after incarceration?
   - What role does school play in shaping their self-concept?

3. **Gender and Reentry**

- What are the distinct reentry experiences of girls and nonbinary youth?

- How do gendered expectations affect reengagement?

4. **Impact of Mentorship Models**
   - What kinds of mentorship (peer, adult, virtual) are most effective?

   - How does identity matching (race, background) influence outcomes?

5. **Teacher Perspectives Post-Training**
   - How do teacher attitudes shift after trauma-informed or reentry training?

   - Does training lead to measurable classroom practice change?

6. **Policy Analysis Across States**
   - What state-level reentry policies are most effective?

   - How do accountability systems impact support for returning youth?

A robust research agenda will not only inform practice, but it will also help hold systems accountable. A Call to Action.

This book began with a story—Jamal, sitting in a windowless classroom in a detention facility, holding a worksheet and wondering whether anyone cared. It ends with an invitation to build school systems where students like Jamal are not forgotten but fiercely supported.

This is not charity work. It is justice work.

"These are our kids," one teacher said. "If we don't make space for them, we are complicit in their disappearance."

CONCLUSION: FROM REENTRY TO RESTORATION

Reentry is not a single moment, it's a journey. It starts behind walls and continues across classrooms, communities, and systems. It asks schools to be more than academic institutions. It asks them to be places of healing, growth, and redemption.

The FIRST plan is a roadmap, but the destination is a reimagined school, where students are not defined by their worst mistakes, but empowered by their deepest potential.

Let us begin that journey, together.

About the Author

Dr. Robert E. Gaines is an educator, school administrator, researcher, and passionate advocate committed to improving outcomes for marginalized youth—especially those affected by the juvenile justice system. With over two decades of experience in urban education, he has served as a teacher, school leader, and district-level administrator, with a focus on educational equity, student reentry, dropout prevention, and restorative justice.

Dr. Gaines holds a doctorate in Educational Leadership and has conducted pioneering research on the reentry experiences of formerly incarcerated high school students. His work seamlessly connects policy with practice, offering actionable strategies for schools and districts aiming to build inclusive, trauma-informed environments that support every learner.

As a practitioner-scholar, Dr. Gaines continues to advise on education policy and consult with schools dedicated to enhancing reentry pathways for youth. *Reentry and Resilience* is his debut book and a reflection of his lifelong mission: to ensure that every student—regardless of their past—has the opportunity to thrive and succeed.